MW01230753

Minute Help Presents:

Liberace

The Unofficial Biography

By Frances Valentino

Minute Help Press

www.minutehelp.com

Table of Contents

Introduction

For the better part of two decades, Liberace was one of the highest-paid entertainers in the world. The classical-turned-pop pianist who made his millions as a brash, bodacious, extravagant onstage spectacle pulled himself up from humble beginnings as the son of Polish and Italian immigrants.

In the 1920s and 1930s, the man who became known as Liberace was a prodigious kid, playing piano to earn enough money to help his family during The Great Depression. In time, he parlayed that natural talent, charisma, street smarts and creativity into a marketable, bankable brand that made an indelible print on pop culture and remained part of the West's collective memory for more than forty years.

Chapter 1: Early Life

When Salvatore Liberace made his way to the United States he was a young Italian immigrant who had left his impoverished home in Formia, Italy with just a few changes of clothes, his French horn and hopes for a better quality of life. A prodigious musician, Salvatore was disciplined about his craft. His sharply honed skills helped him to quickly find work as a musician upon his arrival in the States. In 1906, Salvatore secured a position playing with John Philip Sousa's United States Marine Band. He followed that up by earning steady income as a horn player with a local ensemble in Menasha, Wisconsin where he met his future wife, Frances Zuchowska. Frances was the daughter of Polish immigrant farmers and her family, like Salvatore's family, was quite musical.

In 1909, Salvatore and Frances married and moved to the newly chartered factory city of West Allis, a bustling suburban community in Milwaukee County, on the outskirts of the city. Hundreds of immigrants and their families were moving to West Allis in hopes of earning a living wage working factory jobs at Allis-Chalmers, Kearney & Trecker and the Pawling & Harnischfeger Company. For the time being, Salvatore was content to earn his living as a skilled instrumentalist.

Two years after saying "I do," Salvatore and Frances welcomed their first child, George, into the family, followed by the birth of Angie two years later in 1913. Salvatore's love for music compelled him to train his own children in the discipline so he decided to have George study the violin and Angelina was trained as a classical pianist. During this time, Salvatore himself got steady work playing music in movie theatres for silent films. He eventually won a chair playing with the Milwaukee Philharmonic Orchestra.

By 1919, the Liberaces were preparing to welcome a new set of twins into the family and on May 16, Frances successfully gave birth to two boys. However, when the babies emerged, it became evident that at some point during the pregnancy, something had gone terribly wrong. One of their sons was stillborn, emaciated, likely having starved to death while the other baby boy was born weighing in at an astonishing 13 pounds. Wladziu (pronounced Vla-ja) Valentino Liberace was born with a caul – part of the amniotic sac was still attached to his face at birth. At that time, it was a common belief in many cultures that being born with a caul was a sign of genius, evidence that the child was destined for greatness and would lead a life of distinction. And Wladziu Liberace would certainly prove them right.

Wladziu, called "Walter" by his family and "Lee" by his friends, was the third of four children that Frances and Salvatore had together. The fourth child, Rudolph Valentino Liberace (named for Frances's favorite film star, Rudolph Valentino) was born in 1931. Despite his initial size as an infant, Walter was noticeably weaker than the other neighborhood children. At the age of two, he suffered a vicious bout with pneumonia that left him fighting for his life during a lengthy recovery period. The end result was that he spent a significant portion of his early childhood as a rather frail child when compared to the children around him. The other boys in the neighborhood were typically faster and stronger than Walter and for years, he was subject to frequent bullying, fueled in part by the fact that he also had a speech impediment (the result of learning the speech patterns of his mother's thick Polish accent and his father's pronounced Italian accent) and preferred the fine arts to football. Walter eventually received speech therapy to help smooth out his speech. Throughout his life, Walter maintained a slow, deliberate rhythm to his speech.

Salvatore's reverence for all things music made musicality as much a part of every day life for the Liberace family as dinner conversation. His heavy-handed discipline shaped the Liberace children into strong musicians from their youth. Salvatore was strict about their practice time and he maintained high standards of performance for all three of his children. By the age of four, even young Walter could be found in front of the piano picking out tunes by ear that he had heard his older brother George playing on the violin. By the age of six, Walter was playing tunes in their entirety completely by ear. It was then that Salvatore recognized his son's prodigious talent and set out to find a private instructor who would either take Walter on for free or at a low cost. Salvatore successfully made contact with Florence Kelly, an instructor at the Wisconsin College of Music who had studied with the virtuoso Moriz Rosenthal. Florence agreed to take Walter under her wing and from there Walter studied with Florence for the next ten years.

Where music was concerned, Salvatore spared no expense. By 1925, the financial impact musicianship was having on the Liberace household in the form of music lessons, concert tickets and other costs associated with being a musician was beginning to cause constant conflicts between Salvatore and Frances. Salvatore was no longer able to sustain a family of five on a musician's salary, particularly since jobs for French horn players were becoming increasingly difficult to find. But Salvatore refused to take any other kind of work and scratched and scraped when he could to find the money for musical training for the kids – those were the essentials in his eyes. His wife, on the other hand, thought music lessons and other purchases like the family's phonograph record player were unnecessary luxuries that they simply couldn't afford. Their marriage was in trouble.

For years Salvatore chose to forego work in the factories in favor of unemployment. And his pride for his craft kept him from taking jobs playing pop music over the classics even when silent films were replaced by talking pictures, or "talkies", as the norm in movie theatres. To stave off financial ruin, the Liberaces transformed their tiny home into a neighborhood grocery store and lived in a modest apartment in the back of the house. Many days Frances and the kids worked in the store then grabbed a potato or two from the store shelf for the night's dinner.

In 1926, Florence Kelly helped Walter get a scholarship to study music at the Wisconsin Conservatory of Music in Milwaukee. Kelly taught him to read music and weighted his fingers to help them build strength and speed. Later in life, Walter Liberace held the record for speed with Ripley's Believe it or Not for being able to play 6,000 notes on the piano in just 2 minutes. Walter was able to memorize difficult pieces of music, a feat he demonstrated at home when Salvatore assigned Angie seventeen pages of music from Mendelssohn's *Midsummer Night's Dream* to learn. Angie had trouble learning the piece and after several weeks of practice was disappointed to find that young Walter knew it by heart and worst, he could play it from memory, which he did for their father.

One of Walter's all-time favorite pianists was Polish pianist and former Prime Minister of Poland, Ignace Paderewski. At the age of eight years old, Walter got the opportunity to hear Paderewski perform at the Pabst Theatre in Milwaukee. At his mother's insistent plea, the family got the opportunity to go backstage to meet Paderewski, where Walter was able to perform for him and forge a lasting mentorship with the great virtuoso. After that meeting, Walter's appetite for the piano was insatiable.

By 1929, the Great Depression had settled on households across the nation and the impression left on Walter of the lack and squalor the Depression caused was something that he spent his entire life combating. The Liberaces had closed their neighborhood grocery store and every member of the family was charged with earning money to bring into the house. George gave piano lessons and drove a grocery truck, Angie worked as a secretary and nurse's aide, Frances worked in a cookie factory and embroidery hosiery at night, and young Walter earned a little money washing dishes and playing piano for local dance classes. Occasionally, Walter would have the opportunity to bang out some pop tunes at the local movie house or at a party, but the decision was always served with a sizable helping of contempt and anger from his purist father.

For Walter, playing popular tunes was a way to gain social acceptance. His peers didn't particularly care for the classics, so every chance he got, Walter would show up to play for parties and to take song requests as he played piano in the girls' gymnasium. Sure, he'd throw in a quick minuet or abbreviated concerto once in a while, but for the most part he was becoming known for being able to churn out the hits of the day at will. When he was fourteen years old, Florence Kelly helped Walter to get a contract with a Chicago-based booking agency that kept him busy with engagements at local high schools, colleges, weddings, theatres, live venues and community organizations. Walter also took jobs at speakeasies, stag shows and was even arrested in a couple of raids, but never charged due to his young age.

During his attendance at West Milwaukee High School, Walter Liberace wasn't particularly popular. He was a skilled pianist and growing in popularity as a professional musician, but his classmates found him odd, though he performed well academically. Outside of school, he performed with a musical ensemble called The Mixers. Between the years of 1933 to 1939, the relationship between his mother and father continued to deteriorate and Walter took every opportunity he could to gig if it meant keeping him away from home, and all the more when Walter spotted his father out on a date with a cellist from the Milwaukee symphony, whom he later found out had been his father's mistress for years. Walter felt betrayed and began taking gigs all over the Midwest to keep from coming home.

Of course, by this time Walter was earning enough money to support his mother on his own. Frances and Salvatore divorced in 1941 and Salvatore's presence in Walter's life diminished significantly. Frances moved to Milwaukee and remarried in 1943. Her husband died just two years later.

Chapter 2: Early Career

In 1939, Florence Kelly leveraged her connections to get Walter an opportunity to play as a soloist with the Chicago Symphony during their visit to Milwaukee. That summer, Walter delivered a flawless audition and was hired in as a soloist for the symphony's upcoming performance in Milwaukee in January. In the meantime, Walter continued performing pop music, making appearances at local clubs and playing with the Jay Mills Orchestra. One of Walter's pop performances was broadcast on the radio, causing quite a stir among the administration and talent in the Chicago Symphony. In those days, classical musicians were a lot like Walter's father had been – purists. But Frederick Stock, director of the Chicago Symphony, wasn't going to give up on Walter so easily and despite pressure from other members of the Chicago Symphony, Stock refused to remove Walter from the program. But he did have one requirement - Walter would need to use a stage name to keep his pop persona and his classical career separate until after his performance with the Chicago Symphony. Walter performed as "Walter Buster Keys" for the duration of his contract with the Chicago Symphony, then retired the stage name shortly thereafter and went back to using his own name.

Walter's performance with the Chicago Symphony on January 5, 1940 was a success and helped catapult him into regional fame. He toured the Midwest, pulling more and more away from billing himself as just a classical musician. He refused to become unemployable like his father. Riding on the strong reviews of his performance with the Chicago Symphony in 1940 and encouraged by his brother George, Walter began touring the Midwest as a pop act. Between 1940 and 1942, Walter changed his act in several distinct ways. First, he took the advice of his mentor Paderewski and dropped the word "Walter" from his billing. He began playing under the moniker Liberace. Next, he continued to pay homage to his classic roots, but learned that his adult audience, much like his high school audience years before, preferred pop music with tiny doses of classics every now and then. So he rebranded himself as a pop artist, playing ragtime and boogie woogie to earn more money. Finally, he classed up his act a bit by playing a custom piano and decorating it with a golden candelabrum, which he purchased for $12.50 from a local store.

In 1942, Liberace made his debut in New York, taking work where he could find it in night clubs, hotels and lounges. He had successfully made the transition from classical musician to pop musician, adding whimsy and flair to musical pieces to the pleasure of his audiences. He garnered attention by playing along with a phonograph record, adding live embellishments to tunes that had already been popularized. One of the things that really helped Liberace to woo his audiences was his personable, Midwestern charm. He often engaged with his audience during performances, taking requests and making jokes so that each performance was interactive and not simply a spectacle for the audience to watch. Not only did that interactivity help him to keep the interest of his audience, but it also helped Liberace to keep his energy and enthusiasm up when he played for smaller audiences. A year later, Liberace appeared in two short music video clips called Soundies. He played *Tiger Rag* and *Twelfth Street Rag*.

In 1944, during his travels to perform at the Mount Royal Hotel in Montreal, Liberace received a call from Maxine Lewis, who was the entertainment director at the Hotel Last Frontier. Maxine invited Liberace to perform at their hotel in Vegas and offered to match the amount he was currently being paid by the Mount Royal Hotel. In truth, Liberace was earning about $350 per week playing at the hotel, but he told Maxine that it was $750 per week. She matched it and that began Liberace's lifelong love affair with the Las Vegas strip. At that time, Vegas was a desert town that was building a name for itself with legalized gambling. People were coming from all over the country to have a chance at winning big and Liberace arrived at just the right time to capitalize on the newness, excitement, buzz and growth of Vegas. Liberace wowed his audience the first night. After quickly sizing them up, he was smart enough to remove the classics from his repertoire and focus on just the popular tunes. That night, the value of his contract doubled and he went from making $750 a week to $1,500 a week. Liberace's musical talent, down home charm and boyish good looks brought not just women, but families into the casinos in droves. Both single women and wives loved Liberace and packed his performances every night. Husbands who didn't want to stick around for the show could be found gambling in the casino. Liberace was good for business and eventually was awarded a ten-year contract with the hotel that reflected his value.

Liberace was a media marvel. The press loved him. He was playing the hottest venues in Las Vegas and gaining plenty of publicity for his work as an entertainer. He had garnered positive reviews of his performances in *Variety* as well as *The Chicago Times*. *The Times* went so far as to suggest that Liberace would be great for film. Famed Hollywood manager Seymour Heller saw Liberace's effect on the audience and signed him on the spot, after hearing the dazzling entertainer play just two songs. Heller served as Liberace's manager throughout his career.

Three years after arriving in Las Vegas, Liberace was also playing clubs in the Hollywood area and was a frequent musical guest at parties for such Hollywood heavyweights as Clark Gable, Shirley Temple, J. Paul Getty and Gloria Swanson. He purchased a home in North Hollywood and began billing himself as "Liberace – the most amazing piano virtuoso of the present day." With the help of his manager, his brother George (who was his road manager), and his publicist, Jamie James, Liberace was creating a publicity machine that painted a larger than life image of an amazing entertainer, and Liberace had the technical skill and stage presence to live up to his own hype. He bought a piano to match his own grandiose image and began performing and touring with a gold-leaf Blüthner Grand. While he didn't always play to a packed house when he toured the country, he leveraged his fame and influence as a Las Vegas darling. His act in Las Vegas was spectacular. Liberace began to focus on details like lighting, choreography and stage design to increase his appeal, invent his particular brand of magic and keep his audiences growing and coming back for more.

In 1950, Liberace was extended an invitation to perform for President Harry S. Truman in the East room of the White House and while he reportedly enjoyed the opportunity to perform for the leader of the free world, Liberace also had his sights set on two opportunities he considered even more beneficial to his career – film and television. Liberace made his film debut beside Shelley Winters in *South Sea Sinner* playing a honky-tonk pianist. The movie was no box office smash by any measure, but it served to give Liberace a glimpse into a brighter, much more spectacular future.

Beginning in the 1950s, Liberace began expanding his act to make it more and more extravagant. He went from being a pop musician to being an entertainer, billing himself as "Mr. Showmanship." That began the legend of the character, brand and commodity of Liberace, a legendary persona that made Walter Valentino Liberace a very, very wealthy man.

In just four years, Liberace went from being a Las Vegas act to being a household name. He was in demand across the country as a musician and entertainer. Women adored him. He was the handsome, angel-faced heartthrob to which millions of women - married and single, old and young - flocked every single week to watch his televised program, *The Liberace Show*. He was rich, earning money from his television show, his standing Las Vegas contracts as well as national performances. He was selling out live shows left and right and audiences could not get enough of him.

But along with his growing fame came harsh criticisms from music critics who often claimed his piano playing was subpar, messy and extravagant to the point of being a distraction. Liberace knew how to give his audiences a show and when he performed, he choreographed his stage shows so that only the most interesting parts of each piece were played. He rearranged classics and pop tunes alike so that they were no more than five or six minutes long each. He played classics like they were pop and pop as classics. He didn't adhere to tempo markings on the music and he reinterpreted phrasing at-will, depending on his audience. He added flourishes and runs to tunes that were written simply and simplified more complicated pieces. Such freedom of interpretation left many music critics outraged by his seeming lack of reverence for the aesthetic they thought should have been presented untouched in each piece, particularly classical pieces. Instead Liberace recreated each piece of music in his own image. Many critics agreed that he had no true understanding of music or musicality.

What Liberace did understand was his audience and he was beholden to one aesthetic – putting on a great show for those who came to see him. Liberace knew what his audiences liked and he knew what they didn't like. He knew what would keep them buying tickets to his shows and he knew what wouldn't. He presented himself as an entertainer, a showman whose sole delight was in stirring and satisfying his audience. He didn't end his shows with a bow followed by a hurried scurry offstage. He ended his shows with warmth and familiarity, inviting audience members onstage to engage with him. He shook hands and passed out hugs. He gave quick piano lessons and flirted harmlessly with women who would cherish his playful wink for the rest of their lives. He was loving and charismatic, and that love was returned.

Technical prowess aside, the persona of Liberace – this Midwestern boy who had made it big and who was now sharing his wealth and opulence with the world – was what brought Wladziu Valentino Liberace millions of dollars and unmatched wealth. Between the 1950s and 1970s, Liberace averaged $5 million a year in performance income. He was one of the highest-paid entertainers in the world for two decades straight and certainly the highest-paid pianist in the world.

In a single performance at New York's Madison Square Garden in 1954, Liberace earned an astounding $138,000. As Liberace's fame and wealth exploded, so did his public image. That same year, Liberace played the Hollywood Bowl. His typical ensemble at that time included a black tuxedo and a few pieces of jewelry. Jamie James tells the story that when Liberace was hired to play the Hollywood Bowl, organizers thought it would be a good idea for the entertainer to wear something other than a black tuxedo so that the audience could easily distinguish him from the orchestra. Liberace showed up for the event in a white suit of tails and the press went crazy for him the next day. When Liberace signed the contract to play for the opening of the Riviera Hotel and Casino in Las Vegas, the press immediately wanted to know what he would wear to the gala event and Liberace hadn't even thought about it. Grabbing inspiration from his sister, Angie, who was seated beside him in a gold lamé dress, he flippantly blurted out that he would wear a gold lamé jacket to the opening. He did and it shocked the crowd. And again, the press went crazy for him. From that time on, Liberace began building an eclectic and extravagant wardrobe for the stage that was unmatched by any other entertainer of the day.

By the mid-1950s, Liberace was bringing in upward of $50,000 per week with just his contract with the Riviera Hotel and Casino in Las Vegas. He was earning more than a million dollars per year solely from public appearances and generating millions from television. Liberace had his first home built in the early 1950s and decked the piano-themed home with a piano-shaped pool, plush furniture and lavish antiques. Now in his mid-thirties, Liberace's effeminate qualities, love for jewelry and frequent and often gaudy displays of wealth began to bring into question his sexuality. While he certainly made no claims that he was anything other than heterosexual, the press was well aware that he also hadn't showed much interest in women offstage, not like he had in his playful, friendly jabs onstage.

Perhaps in an attempt to combat the rumors, Liberace began a very public love affair with an aspiring actress who lived just across the road from him. Joanne Rio was a gorgeous, girl next door type with a kind of fresh-faced glamour that was well-suited for Liberace's image at the time. An aspiring actress, she was in the entertainment business and had been in close contact with Liberace in the past. In fact, he had previously used Joanne in his stage shows. She was beautiful, likeable and had a dynamite figure. There was no doubt that the two could have been involved. Whether or not they actually were is still a mystery.

For weeks, the press loved Liberace and Joanne as a couple. Pictures of the two of them together were snapped frequently as they made their rounds at all the right Hollywood parties and hot spots. They were even seen in public holding hands and kissing. Within just a few months, Liberace and Joanne were reportedly engaged. When pressed for a wedding date, Liberace insisted he would not marry Joanne for another year, but he hoped she would wait patiently for him to finish up his touring over the next twelve months. And Joanne sang his praises by telling millions of American women that Liberace was the perfect all-American man – sweet and thoughtful, loving and respectful. She went on to say that if it was God's will, they would indeed be married.

The backlash from Liberace's female audience was immediately felt. Thousands of letters came pouring in from broken-hearted gals all over the country, some of whom believe they had as much a claim to him as Joanne. The fan mail ran the gamut of emotions from sadness and dismay to congratulatory glee to downright outrage. The ladies were inconsolable. Concerned that his engagement would affect his fan base and ultimately his bottom line, Liberace began to reconsider his engagement to Joanne, or at least that's what Seymour Heller said. Heller insisted that it was Liberace who decided to break off the engagement, but Liberace asked him to deliver the news to Joanne, which he did as a friend.

To this day, there are many people who think Liberace's relationship with Joanne Rio was little more than another well-orchestrated performance.

Chapter 3: The Liberace Show

As luck would have it, Liberace's imminent rise to fame coincided with two of the country's most magnificent innovations.

First, the recent development of Las Vegas, Nevada as a tourist attraction, gambling center and anything goes entertainment oasis in the middle of the desert was the perfect place to build Liberace's career. Las Vegas specialized in fulfilling fantasies. The stage shows were extravagant, the city never slept and as far as people were concerned, it was possible to arrive in Las Vegas a pauper and leave Las Vegas a prince. Liberace and his nonstop publicity machine were busy creating the perfect pop culture icon in his Mr. Showmanship stage personality. The ongoing engagements in Vegas were helping Liberace to hone the experience of his live performance while keeping his pockets lined with more money than he had time to spend.

Second, families all across America were adding televisions to their living room décor. The television was new and for Liberace, the time was right to use the newness of television to grow his career exponentially. And that's just what it did. Liberace was made for television. While most musicians of the time found recording and radio were the natural progression from live local performances, Liberace was way ahead of the game. He understood that his strength was in the visual aspect of his live shows. Women loved his baby-faced good looks. Men and women alike were entertained and engaged by his theatrics when he played. He was fun to watch. Working the Vegas audiences had taught him the ways he could afford to take some risks in his performance. He learned that musicianship is a legacy. Showmanship is a living. Radio simply would not do Liberace justice. People needed to see him. People *wanted* to see him. So being the shrewd and bold businessman that he was, Liberace chose to forego records, bypass radio and instead focus on building his on-screen repertoire. He had done a movie. Now, he wanted to focus on television.

Liberace had several early television appearances before he had his own show. He appeared on *The Kate Smith Show* and *Cavalcade of Stars* with Jackie Gleason and the experiences left much to be desired. That was his take on it, at least. As a musical guest, Liberace was not in control of how his performance looked when it aired, nor could he control the amount of his performance that was shown. He had been very deliberate, very hands-on in shaping his career to that point and he certainly wasn't willing to relinquish control to pursue television. Instead of appearing as a musical guest on the popular television shows of the day, Liberace decided that he wanted his own show. This way, he could control how he appeared, just like he did with his other live performances.

When Liberace first decided to do his own show, Seymour Heller put him in a car and drove him around Beverly Hills, the world-renowned affluent suburb just west of Los Angeles. Afterward, Heller drove Liberace around the San Fernando Valley, a series of working class communities north of L.A. These represented two distinct demographics and Heller asked Liberace what the difference was between the two. After a moment of thought, Liberace noticed that the homes in the valley had TV antennas while the ones in Beverly Hills didn't. Liberace had identified his audience and went about creating programming that would appeal to the working class public.

In 1952, the first episodes of *The Liberace Show* aired locally in Los Angeles. It was just 15 minutes long and within just a few weeks, *The Liberace Show* proved to be a big hit. The show was the highest-rated local show in the L.A. market and drove ticket sales for Liberace's live appearance at the Hollywood Bowl. In fact, by the time he hit the stage at the Hollywood Bowl, his concert was completely sold out. The local success of *The Liberace Show* in the competitive L.A. market paved the way for the show to debut nationally as a summer replacement for *The Dinah Shore Show*.

When *The Liberace Show* premiered, television was still very new and there really weren't too many hard and fast rules for how a performer was to behave on camera. Liberace used that newness to his advantage and created a familial atmosphere that lent itself well to his natural onstage warmth and charm. Somehow, he was able to successfully bridge the gap between his in-studio performance and his home viewing audience. He catered to the tastes, whims and desires of his audience by engaging them. He treated his on-air performances like he did his on-stage performances. He laughed and joked with the camera, chatted, winked at viewers, introduced them to his family members who were all a part of the show (or at least in the studio audience) and worked to make even his on-camera appearance look and feel like a face-to-face with him. In a very short time, the Liberace experience went from being restricted to Las Vegas lounges to being in tens of millions of living rooms across America.

Liberace's older brother George was the band director and was often featured playing violin on the show. His mother Frances usually greeted the television audience from her seat in the very front row of the studio audience. Much like he did during live performances, Liberace used dramatic lighting and exaggerated hand movements to visually engage his audience. He was enthusiastic, pleasing to look at and pleasing to listen to. He beamed at the camera and made it seem as if he was having more fun playing than the viewers could ever have watching him. The flexibility of television provided him the option to do "camera tricks" as well so he incorporate costume changes and on-screen split images for the home audience to enjoy.

The weekly Sunday broadcast of *The Liberace Show* was a date that many women were faithful to keep. America had its very first TV idol. *The Liberace Show* launched Liberace into superstardom. The tabloids couldn't get enough of him. He had 200 official fan clubs with a quarter million fans. Thousands of fan letters were pouring into the studio every single week. Valentines Day cards topped 20,000 annually.

In his first two years doing *The Liberace Show*, Walter Liberace earned $7 million with an 80% residual negotiated on the profits for all future reruns. Not only that, but his charm and accessibility made him the perfect spokesman for dozens and dozens of goods and services. Advertisers were not quick to rush to television, but Liberace seemed to understand two things – his show needed sponsors to continue airing and he could sell most anything to an audience if he tried. The proof was in the pudding. Immediately after singing the bank's praises on his show, Citizen's Bank saw more than half a million dollars in new deposits. Advertising worked. And Liberace had proven that he could influence the masses. The advertising dollars poured in and Liberace began endorsing hundreds of products on the air, even to the dismay of entertainment critics who began to see him as a smiling televised peddler of goods with very little discrimination about what he chose to sell.

The Liberace Show featured Mr. Showmanship himself playing a varied repertoire of songs, making conversation, offering observations and even doing a bit of light dancing. He played the classics – well, his version of the classics – and he incorporated ragtime and boogie woogie into the play list. He also played show tunes, music from popular film scores and even introduced a bit of world music on the program. *The Liberace Show* opened and closed the same way for its entire duration. At the end of each show, Liberace signed off singing I'll Be Seeing You as his theme song.

After his much publicized debut in the gold lamé jacket at the Riviera in the mid-1950s, Liberace also began dressing more boldly to satisfy his audiences' taste for the outrageous. His wardrobe became more and more flamboyant.. Liberace could be found wearing the most stunning jackets and robes. He didn't shy away from accessories like boas and he spared no expense in having his clothes designed. Whatever he could imagine, he commissioned. Sponsors gave him jewelry, gifts, clothes and cars in exchange for advertising time on his popular television show. Liberace made good use of what was given, often flaunting his wares in front of his adoring audience. They rarely took offense. Liberace just had a way of being both haughty and lowly in the same breath. It was nothing for him to take time during a show to let female audience members ogle a pinky ring or a diamond bracelet. He had no qualms about discussing how such pieces came to be his and as his wealth grew, so did his extravagance both on camera and off camera.

Soon both his live performances and his broadcast shows titillated audiences with showgirls, jugglers, more costume changes, special celebrity guests, light shows and water fountains whose movements seemed to be controlled by the music Liberace played. And of course, Mr. Showmanship also had to up his game. Several times he started the show by flying in over the crowd on a wire, one of his gorgeous capes flapping gently behind him.

The Liberace Show aired from 1952 to 1955. By 1954, *The Liberace Show* was being carried by more stations than I Love Lucy. At its height, the show drew 30 million viewers a week. There were 217 American stations broadcasting the program. One station, WPIX in New York, ran *The Liberace Show* 10 times a week. *The Liberace Show* also aired in 20 foreign countries. It was one of the first American television programs to make it to British television, airing on Sunday afternoons by Lew Grades Associated TeleVision. In a very short time, not only did Liberace become a bona fide super star in America, but he was also growing in popularity overseas. The show helped him to sell out venues all over the country.

Liberace had successfully thrust himself into the public consciousness. By 1955, he was arguably the biggest star in America. He was the highest-paid entertainer in Vegas and one of the highest-paid entertainers in the world. As his fame grew the paradox that existed between the character he had created and the man he really was became more and more apparent. Liberace the superstar clamored for the brilliance and influence of the limelight. He walked with a sort of heel-forward strike on stage. Lee, as his friends knew him, didn't like interviews. He didn't care much to be photographed and he actually walked with a kind of heavy-footed shuffle in private. While Liberace graced the covers of tabloids and kept his name in the paper with well-orchestrated media stunts to keep eyes on his television show, Lee never wanted to be recorded. He thought the idea of a camera or recording device capturing one of his mistakes for all posterity was distasteful. On the show, Liberace would make several wardrobe changes to wow his audience. Lee would wear the same clothes at home for weeks at a time. Liberace was sociable, chatty and funny. He naturally – seemingly without much thought - drew people to him. He would willingly and freely show them his heart and they would respond favorably. Lee was very private and could be described as distant. At parties, he would stand in the corner and wait for others to approach him. He was a genius and far more calculating than naturally loving. Liberace had a beautiful, gentle smile that seemed to be an authentic expression of the warm and loving man who showed up on stage every night. As soon as he turned away, however, the smile would fall, not fade and not reappear until the next time Liberace was "on." Liberace was a flirty, charming All-American Mama's boy who loved women and was waiting on the right girl to come alone. Lee did love Mom, but he was also gay.

Chapter 4: Later Career

When *The Liberace Show* went off the air in 1955, Liberace was at the height of his fame. He was swimming in money from live performances and television work. His performance contract with the Riviera in Vegas was earning him $50,000 per week, a stark contrast from the $50,000 per year he earned when he arrived in Vegas just a decade before. The television show had worked wonders for his recording career, which he had essentially put on hold in order to do television. That turned out to be a wise decision. In fact, between 1947 and 1951, Liberace had recorded and released 10 records. By 1954, he had a total of 60 records to his credit and had sold more than 400,000 albums and 300,000 copies of "Ave Maria." Much like his live performances, Liberace's recordings included a varied selection of tunes, from "Hello Dolly" to colorful interpretations of classical pieces rearranged to suit Liberace's style and appeal to his audience.

In the mid-1950s, Liberace's performance schedule was showing no signs of letting up and he continued to wow audiences across the nation with his spectacular costumes, over-the-top concerts and his folksy personality. Liberace also took a chance on another movie role and starred in *Sincerely Yours* with Dorothy Malone. The film didn't do well at the box office, but was able to find new life in the late 50s and 60s when it was added to the television's movie programming after Warner Brothers took it out of the theatres.

In 1956, Liberace embarked on a well-received international tour, which included an engagement in Havana, Cuba followed by a European tour. He arrived in London in September of 1956 to droves of female fans and mounds and mounds of press – good and bad. During his tour, Liberace also got the opportunity to meet with Pope Pius XII, an event he later recalled as one of the highlights of his career and of his life.

Despite having launched a successful European tour, by 1957 Liberace's popularity was starting to wane. He was all over the television and all over the papers and tabloids. He still packed venues in Vegas, but his record sales were in steady decline and his bookings were down for his national performance dates. Coinciding with his libel case against the UK's *Daily Mirror* in 1956 and a similar case against Confidential in 1957 whom he was suing for insinuating that he was gay, Liberace decided to rein in his onstage persona a little and in 1958, Liberace spent several months as a clean-cut, buttoned-down performer like he had been in the beginning of his career, before the television show and before his splashy debut at the Riviera in Vegas four years before. Ticket sales and bookings immediately began to plummet. He even made an attempt to re-launch *The Liberace Show* on ABC's daytime programming format with a less flamboyant version of himself and the show was a big flop and off the air within six months. Between 1958 and 1959, Liberace earned half of what he had with his previous over-the-top image. So immediately following the *Daily Mirror* trial, he again began appearing in public in the spectacular clothes for which he had become known and went to work rebuilding his reputation and popularity by playing small venues all over the country, doing guest spots on television programs and increasing his appearance schedule. Liberace made television appearances on *The Ed Sullivan Show*, *The Tonight Show* with Jack Paar, *Person to Person*, Jack Benny, *The Ford Show* and Red Skelton. He was often featured poking fun at himself and his own extravagance and he had several memorable and even hilarious exchanges on both prime time and day time television.

In 1960, Liberace received a star on the Hollywood Walk of Fame for his contributions to television. In that same year, he also made a return trip to Great Britain to take part in the first ever televised presentation of *The Royal Variety Show* for Queen Elizabeth II. Liberace always made it a point to learn the names of the staff and crew with whom he worked. That effort served him well as he was usually able to recall their names when he worked with them later on in his career. People grew to love working with Liberace. On his birthday in 1960, Liberace took the stage at the London Palladium to perform alongside Sammy Davis Jr. and Nat King Cole. The show aired on television six days later.

In November 1963, Liberace was checked into the hospital with renal failure thought to be the result of inadvertent poisoning from inhaling cleaning fluid. The doctors did not expect him to survive the damage that had been done to his kidneys. Liberace, convinced that he was dying, immediately called in his family and closest friends and began giving away all of his possessions. Thankfully, he was able to fully recover after several weeks and returned to the Las Vegas strip with a renewed sense of purpose and a commitment to creating the most fantastic live performances any audience had ever seen. The new and improved Liberace delivered more passion, more enthusiasm, more glamour and more bang for the buck. His costumes were more imaginative with pronounced flairs of exoticism. His jewelry was even more dynamic and stunning than anything he had ever worn before. He began the tradition of being chauffeured onstage in a Rolls Royce and he added more eye candy to create an even greater spectacle for his audience.

Liberace choreographed his live shows to include showgirls, dancers, animals and novelty acts. He began debuting new talent during his shows, pulling operatic singers from the local opera companies and classically trained dancers from local ballet companies. He also made it a point to introduce new and exciting talent on his show, which included the likes of Barbara Streisand early on in her career. He used his live shows as a way to launch the careers of lesser known and unknown talent. Liberace always favored children and often incorporated them into his live shows as well.

Liberace's new found enthusiasm reignited his interest in both movies and television as well. In 1965, he appeared in *When the Boys Meet the Girls* starring Connie Francis then took another small role a year later in the film adaptation of *The Loved One*. *The Loved One* was the only movie in which Liberace was cast where he did not play piano. 1966 was also the year when Liberace appeared in a two-part story on *Batman* with Adam West in dual roles playing a concert pianist and his evil twin. Those two episodes were the highest-rated story ever to air on Batman. His continued success on television included serving as Red Skelton's summer replacement on his variety show, appearing on *The Monkees* as himself, an appearance on *Here's Lucy* and a guest starring role on *The Muppets* where he played several numbers on the piano, including *Chopsticks.*

From childhood, Liberace loved to cook. Celebrities like Mike Douglas and Phyllis Diller have gone on record as being partakers in some of Lee's masterful late night dinners, many of them created using just a small burner and a few key ingredients. Liberace was well-known as a man who knew his way around a kitchen and by all accounts he was a fantastic cook. Of course, he found a way to market that skill. In 1970, Liberace published the first of several cookbooks. *Liberace Cooks* was coauthored by Carol Truax, and is by far, Liberace's most famous cookbook and his best-selling cookbook. Liberace's recipes were also included in *Cookbook of the Stars* along with treats from Mary Tyler Moore, Bing Crosby and Lana Turner.

Liberace also published the first of three autobiographies in 1973. *Liberace: An Autobiography* was followed up with *The Things I Love* in 1976 and *The Wonderful Private World of Liberace* in 1986. His other commercial ventures included an antique shop, a retail mall, a line of men's clothing and a motel chain.

Throughout the 1970s and the 1980s, Liberace still ranked as one of the highest paid musicians in the country. In 1978 the Guinness Book of World Records listed Liberace as the world's highest paid musician. His live shows at the Las Vegas Hilton and Lake Tahoe were raking in $300,000 a week, putting his earnings well over a million dollars a month. The shows were televised and broadcast on CBS in 1979.

In 1977, Liberace founded the Liberace Foundation for the Performing and Creative Arts, which was created to provide talented young performers the same opportunity he had been provided when he received a scholarship to study at the Wisconsin Conservatory of Music in the 1920s. Over the course of its duration, the scholarship has provided millions of dollars in scholarship money.

In 1979, Liberace also opened The Liberace Museum in Las Vegas after failed attempts to open the museum first in Los Angeles and again near his hometown of West Allis, Wisconsin. The museum was opened almost on a humbug. Liberace decided to begin displaying his valuables, collectibles and antiques after a relative commented that his house was like a museum. He first decided to just stick items conspicuously in the window of his Hollywood home, but the traffic congestion caused by the display drove his neighbors to complain. Next, he found a separate facility in Wisconsin that he thought would be the perfect site for his museum, but while the purchase of the property was still in the works, a local university bought the land he was planning to secure. Finally, on April 15, 1979, Liberace opened The Liberace Museum in Las Vegas, as part of his retail plaza that also houses his restaurant. The museum houses Liberace's dazzling array of antiques, collectibles and costumes that he had accumulated over the years. A separate building housed his cars and an astounding collection of pianos, including a piano that was previously owned by Frédéric Chopin and another that was owned by George Gershwin. The museum also housed a beautiful inlaid and ormolued Louis XV desk that Liberace himself used to pay his bills and write letters. The museum closed in October 2010, but while it was open, profits were used to fund Liberace Foundation for the Performing and Creative Arts.

In the 1980s, Liberace saw a resurgence in his popularity as a whole new generation of fans discovered the magic of Liberace. His renewed popularity shined the limelight on him yet again and in addition to earning money from his exciting live performances, the renewed buzz about Liberace gave him the chance to take his place in front of the camera. Liberace he secured guest spots on some of the most popular television shows of the day including *Saturday Night Live* and *The Tonight Show*, this time with Johnny Carson. Liberace even left his mark on what was then the World Wrestling Federation by serving as a guest time keeper in the main even of the very first *Wrestlemania*. In 1982, Liberace took center stage at the Academy Awards to present the award for and perform selections from the nominees for Best Original Score. As was his way, he won the crowd by playing a string of wonderful selections while chatting and joking with the audience.

Liberace, the quintessential showman finished his career with a high-energy series of live shows at New York's Radio City Music Hall. In 1984, 1985 and 1986, Liberace delivered stellar performances during three extended engagements at the famed concert hall. He sold out 56 straight shows to wrap up a remarkable career that began in the 1930s and stretched into the 1980s. Liberace's final concert performance was on November 2, 1986. The great Liberace – Mr. Showmanship - finally retired from live performances after his Radio City shows. What a fitting end to an amazing onstage career.

In a final television performance, Liberace appeared on The Oprah Winfrey Show just a few months after the show first debuted. There the entertainer appeared in a tailored suit, soberly discussing his career and his life in retirement. Liberace was charming and forthright with very little of his trademark showmanship.

Chapter 5: Lawsuits

In the fall of 1956, Liberace was in the midst of a European tour, capitalizing on the fame he built with *The Liberace Show*. His arrival in London was met by the frenzied screams and wails of adulation from a crowd of women who had fallen in love with the handsome and outlandish thirty-something American entertainer who had been gracing their television screens on Sunday afternoons. The day after Liberace's arrival, William Connor, author of the popular *Daily Mirror* column "Cassandra" wrote a scathing, albeit clever commentary on Liberace's long awaited trek to Great Britain. The column focused on Liberace's sexuality and without directly identifying him as homosexual, Connor delivered a descriptive, biting, well-written piece that pointed the reader toward Liberace's sexual orientation and did well to leave *Daily Mirror* readers wondering if Liberace was, in fact, gay.

Well, there was one thing Liberace never stood for and that was bowing to anything or anyone who would serve to compromise his career or his ability to earn a good living. Despite the rumors that abounded about Liberace's sexuality both in the United States and abroad, there was nothing in the performer's public persona that would allow Connor the leverage to accuse Liberace of being gay. Fearing that the accusation would weaken his fan base that had always been mostly women, Liberace filed a libel suit against the *Daily Mirror.* The press loved this case. It had Hollywood scandal written all over it, ripe with celebrity, money and even sex. The topic of homosexuality in the 1950s was still so taboo that when Liberace's libel case hit the press, many newspapers were printing the word for the first time. Even still, some avoided printing the word altogether and opted instead for colloquialisms.

Liberace appeared in court on June 8, 1959, flawlessly manicured and dressed in a simple tailored suit. Armed with a British lawyer whom he barely knew and in whom he hadn't much faith, the case, for Liberace, was about his freedom to a solid brand that he had built and fortified over the past decade. Liberace took the stand to present his case. The entertainer answered questions, offered insights and most importantly, denied that he was gay. After only 3 ½ hours of deliberation, the jury came back with a verdict in his favor, awarding him $22,400 plus court costs, the largest libel award in UK history at that time.

A year before winning his case in the UK, Liberace also went to war against the tabloid *Confidential*, filing a $25 million libel suit against them as well for a similar infraction. In 1957, *Confidential* also implied he was gay in a cover story they ran. The verdict of that case was in Liberace's favor as well. With two wins under his belt, the smart and bold performer was able to keep other publications who perhaps would have submitted a similar opinion to the public for review from ever treading on that territory.

It wasn't until 1982 when Liberace was hit with a $112 million palimony suit in a California courtroom that the cat was truly out of the bag. For years, Mr. Showmanship had had a live-in lover in Scott Thorson, a handsome young man who had worked for years as Liberace's chauffeur and bodyguard. Thorson alleged that he and Liberace had been living together as lovers for five years before Liberace had him forcibly removed from their home. Thorson also alleged that Liberace had paid to have his young lover's face reconstructed to look like a younger version of his own. The papers went wild with the news, particularly because Thorson's attorney had insisted he file a palimony suit against the entertainer who for decades had insisted he was straight. Even amidst the controversy, Liberace still held firm that he was not homosexual and that Thorson was little more than a disgruntled former employee. The presiding judge threw out the palimony case, saying that Thorson's claim that he was also on the payroll made him more of a prostitute than a loving partner. Eventually, Liberace and Thorson settled the dispute in 1986. Thorson was awarded $95,000, two cars and two pet dogs.

In truth, Liberace was gay and hiding his sexuality was a lifelong battle for him. In winning the Cassandra Case, as it later became known, Liberace relinquished the freedom to eventually acknowledge his sexual orientation and come out, if not for fear of losing his loyal female fans, then for fear of being charged with perjury since he had denied under oath that he was gay. His public life and his private life were two conflicting worlds that Lee Liberace carefully constructed. He never stopped working to ensure the two worlds did not collide. In the end though, it is his extravagance for which he is remembered, as well as the secrets he tried so unsuccessfully to hide.

Chapter 6: Later Life

As early as the 1950s, Liberace began entertaining men at his homes in Malibu and Las Vegas. After winning libel cases against both the UK's *Daily Mirror* and Confidential, his older brother and road manager, George did not think it was in good form for the entertainer to be so careless. He thought Liberace was inviting trouble by inviting virtual strangers into his life and his bed. George accused his brother of being reckless and used strong language to try to persuade Liberace that he needed to curb his appetite and behave more responsibly. The disagreement caused Liberace to fire his brother on the spot. He soon rehired George after their mother, Frances, intervened by refusing to attend any of Liberace's public appearances. For years to come, the relationship between Liberace and his brother was strained, but they were eventually able to repair it.

In the ensuing years, Liberace worked hard to balance his public persona with his actual person, keeping his personal life and private struggles largely away from public view. He was fine leaving the public and the media to speculate on their own. That is, as long as their words didn't put a dent in his onstage persona or compromise his pocketbook in any way, the star was fine to let them talk. By the 1970s, the Liberace brand had made its way off the stage and onto television, movies and books. The king of bling had carved a nice little niche for himself of indulgence and opulence that he parlayed into a restaurant, motel chain and men's clothing line. The days of struggling to get people to remember his name were long gone and he was now concerned with building an empire.

Off stage, Lee cultivated a community of paying it forward and giving back. He loved to shop and would often shop for his family and friends. When his publicist Jamie James first moved to the Los Angeles area, Lee helped him to find the quaint two story apartment that Jamie would eventually call home. After seeing the apartment, Lee suspected Jamie would like it and encouraged him to sign a lease. Jamie did eventually take the apartment but working long days kept him from nesting. The apartment remained barren. One day, Jamie got a call from Lee asking him if he could store a few things in Jamie's place. When Jamie arrived home that evening, the apartment was fully furnished and Lee had taken the time to figure out what he thought Jamie would like, save a few outrageous knickknacks here and there.

Lee's sister, Angelina reported not having to go shopping for years and years because Lee would buy so many clothes for Angie and their mother that there were literally items hanging in both their closets with the tags still attached. In Lee's mind, keeping his family close to him – working with them and taking care of them – was the perfect reality. It was the reality he wanted to create to make up for the lean years during the Depression when they had to go without. Off stage Lee was shy and withdrawn. He was quiet and thoughtful and the comfort of being surrounded with those he loved and trusted was essential for him.

Liberace's mother, Frances passed away in 1980 and Lee took his mother's death extremely hard. A few short years later, George died of leukemia in Las Vegas on October 16, 1983. George had been Lee's brother, longtime supporter, road manager, conscience and cheerleader for years. Toward the end of his life, Lee asked his brother to manage The Liberace Museum with his lovely wife, Dora. After George's death, Dora managed The Liberace Museum in her husband's stead until her death in 1996.

For Liberace, the spirit of giving back and paying it forward was essential to his career as well as in private life. Lee considered the creation of the Liberace Foundation to be one of his greatest accomplishments. He designed the program to offer talented musicians the chance to pursue academic endeavors by providing financially disadvantaged high school students the money to attend college. As well, he wanted the program to help undiscovered talent get the opportunity to gain artistic exposure.

In the 1980s, The Liberace Museum was drawing upwards of 50,000 to 100,000 annual visitors through its doors and Liberace structured his business so that much of the money generated by the museum was used to fund the scholarship program sponsored by the Liberace Foundation, which was a non-profit organization headquartered in Las Vegas. In fact, all of the "happy happys" (the name Lee gave to the antiques and prized possessions which populated his museum), were owned and controlled by The Liberace Foundation.

Privately, Lee fulfilled his desire for companionship by adopting dozens of dogs, taking on various male suitors and then co-habiting with Scott Thorson, a handsome young man who had been hired in as Liberace's driver and bodyguard. Thorson and Lee met in 1976 when Thorson was a high school student in California. When Thorson graduated the following year, he got back in touch with Liberace and the superstar put Thorson on the payroll. Thorson worked various positions, filling in as sort of a personal assistant to perform whatever tasks Liberace needed done at the time. He worked in Liberace's act as a dancer and he was the driver who drove Mr. Showmanship on stage in his glimmering Rolls Royce to open the show. He accompanied Liberace to parties and was his nightlife companion and bodyguard for years. Out of the limelight though, Thorson was also Lee's live-in lover, allegedly from the age of 17 until he was 22 years old.

The relationship started out innocently enough, according to Thorson, whose 1988 tell-all book *Behind the Candelabra: My Life with Liberace* chronicles the evolution of his relationship with the superstar. Thorson came from a broken home and when he met Liberace he was actually in foster care. Thorson thought Liberace was poised to be something of a father figure for him. There was even talk of Liberace adopting the young man. But the relationship quickly turned romantic.

Scott Thorson and Liberace were together for years and Thorson maintains that the personal and work relationship between them often merged. Thorson was both bodyguard and limo driver. He was companion and employee. He was lover and son and according to him, he was contracted to be both. Thorson's employment contract came with built-in perks. In addition to his staff pay, Thorson received lavish gifts including expensive cars, clothes and plenty of cash as needed. Lee even went so far as to have Thorson's face restructured to look more like his own, so that they would look more like father and son, according to Thorson. Liberace had Thorson's nose redone, his cheekbones raised and chin implants installed. According to Thorson, that's also when the relationship changed. Thorson was prescribed post-surgery medications designed to help him manage the pain. While he initially used the drugs to dull the pain from the surgery, his reliance on the drugs quickly transitioned into addiction that it took him years to overcome. Thorson said it was around this time that he lost interest in maintaining a sexual relationship with Liberace, who he claimed was extremely promiscuous. Liberace's sexual appetite and popularity frequently afforded him the chance to pursue multiple sexual relationships with other men. When the sex stopped Thorson said he was forcibly removed from the home that he had shared with Lee for five years.

The ordeal was handled quietly for the first year, but the entire affair exploded into the media in 1982 when Scott Thorson filed a palimony suit against Liberace. The newspapers and tabloids raged with this newfound proof that Liberace really was gay and that the rumors that had surrounded the pianist for decades had been spot-on. Liberace steadily denied the claims that he and Scott Thorson were involved in a romantic relationship. He maintained that Thorson was nothing more than an employee. It took nearly four years to finally settle the palimony case. In 1986, Thorson and Liberace were finally able to reconcile and settle the case. According to Thorson, It was not his intention to file a palimony suit. His lawyer had suggested the palimony suit. But Thorson said he wanted to settle the case because Liberace was so sick.

By 1986, rumors about Liberace's deteriorating health began to circulate. Those who knew Lee personally and even some who had worked with him before reported being able to tell the difference between the Liberace they knew and the thinning, subdued man who was showing up at engagements in the mid-1980s. Liberace still gave an impassioned performance, but offstage he was tired, ragged and withdrawn. Hollywood was still aflutter with the recent "outing" and death of Rock Hudson in October 1985. When it was announced that Rock Hudson had died of AIDS, the announcement coincided with confirmations that he was also secretly gay. Like Rock Hudson, Liberace's appearance changed dramatically in a very short time. Rumors began circulating about Liberace, who had always been a healthy, sizable man standing about six feet tall and weighing in at a little over 200 pounds. Liberace's public appearances in 1986 showed the entertainer low key and noticeably thinner.

Both Liberace and his management denied that Mr. Showmanship had AIDS, even amidst the recent controversy with the palimony case. He said that he had been on the watermelon diet and it had made him very sick and at the time of his appearance, he was still recovering from the dangerous effects of the diet. By the close of 1986, Liberace was completely absent from the public eye. In August, he fulfilled his last Vegas contract with a two-week engagement at Caesars Palace. In the fall, he wrapped up the third years of extended engagements at Radio City Music Hall. In mid-November, Liberace made his final public appearance on the Oprah Winfrey Show, where he played a little piano and answered questions about his public and private life.

On February 4, 1987, Liberace died at his home in Palm Springs, surrounded by family and close friends. He was 67 years old. It was known that Liberace had suffered from heart disease and emphysema throughout most of the 1980s, so it was no surprise that his doctor filed a death certificate which stated that Liberace had died from heart failure caused by brain inflammation. In accordance with his wishes, Liberace's body was transported from his home in Palm Springs to the Forest Lawn Mortuary in Los Angeles for cremation. Before the body could be cremated, Riverside County Coroner Ray Carrillo called for an autopsy of the body and the authorities were dispatched to make sure Liberace's body was returned to Palm Springs for an official autopsy.

Against the wishes of his sister Angie, Liberace's body was transported back to the Riverside County Coroner's Office, a police chopper flying overhead to make sure the body arrived. The media swarmed the coroner's office. Ray Carrillo claimed to have fielded some 2,300 calls in just two days as media folks from all over the world tried to get the first word on what killed the talented and irrepressible superstar, Liberace.

Liberace's management team, publicist and family stood by helplessly as the reputation and image Liberace spent a lifetime building was about to be torn down by what many in Liberace's camp thought was a no name country coroner looking for his fifteen minutes of fame. The circus caused by Carrillo's decision to autopsy Liberace forced them to put up police tape to keep the media out of the building. Finally, Carrillo made the announcement in a series of press conferences that Liberace had, in fact tested positive for AIDS antibodies. The pianist had died of pneumonia that was complicated by AIDS. At that time, having AIDS was equivalent to being gay. And just that fast, Liberace's private life was exposed, messily and abruptly in front of the world.

After the spectacle, after the headlines and the news footage, Liberace's body was entombed at Forest Lawn Memorial Park in the Hollywood Hills.

Chapter 7: Legacy after Death

The life, business and legacy that Wlaziu Valentino Liberace was able to build during his lifetime left a permanent mark on the entertainment industry. It may be true that Liberace won't go down in history as the greatest pianist of the 20th century, but Liberace's fingerprint is all over pop music and pop culture today. He was America's first TV heartthrob, the country's first one-name pop star, he headed up the first television ad campaign and he was the first in a string of top-grossing entertainers who have successfully leveraged onstage alter-egos to amass great amounts of wealth. It has also been said that Liberace was the first obviously (though maybe not openly) gay entertainer on television.

Whether loved or hated, Liberace certainly made an impact. The entertainer sold 60 million records over the course of his career, earned six gold records, two Emmys and has stars on both the Hollywood Walk of Fame and the Palm Springs Walk of Fame. He has been voted Instrumentalist of the Year, Best Dressed Entertainer and has held world records both for his technical skill and his earning power. In 1990, he was posthumously inducted into the Milwaukee Hall of Fame and in 1999, the Casino Hall of Fame.

Since its inception in 1977, The Liberace Foundation has awarded thousands of financial scholarships amounting to multiple millions of dollars in funds being distributed to talented students of music. In October 2012, The Foundation filed bankruptcy protection in a fight to manage the assets and liabilities left by The Liberace Museum since its closure in October 2010.

Liberace's life and persona have spawned three autobiographies, eight biographies, two television movies, a BBC documentary, one stage play and a catalogue of other creative works by artists spanning a wide range of tastes and influences. His name and legacy have even made it into the lyrics of the hip hop track *Stunt 101* by 50 cent's group G-Unit. In 2007, The Liberace Foundation collaborated with Pittsburgh-based shoe company Kashi Kicks to release the Liberace shoe to honor of the "King of Bling" with a selection of boldly colored, glittery, piano-theme tennis shoes.

The film adaptation of Scott Thorson's 1988 biography, *Behind the Candelabra: My Life with Liberace* is scheduled to air on HBO in February 2013 with an all-star cast of Michael Douglas as Liberace, Matt Damon as Thorson and Debbie Reynolds as Frances Liberace.

Liberace wanted to be remembered for his musicality. He wanted to be remembered for his determination to etch out a corner of beauty in a world that is wrought with ugliness. That tenderness, that loveliness has always been Liberace's primary offering. Audiences loved him because they were intrigued by his ability to recreate for them a word that was beautiful and carefree – whether that world existed for 15 minutes on a local L.A. broadcast or for two hours on a Vegas stage. The impression he made on his live audiences, his television audiences and the world lingers and people are still intrigued with Mr. Showmanship. There is a certain staying power and permanence to the legend of Liberace.

Conclusion

From the first time young Walter played the piano to earn money to help out his family to very last bow the great entertainer Liberace took on a Vegas stage, fifty seven years passed. It is often said that Liberace's career spanned four decades, but any struggling musician can tell you that you officially make the ranks of pro when you can get paid for your work. Walter "Lee" Liberace built a legendary musical career and a successful entertainment empire. He will be remembered for more than just the scandal and the secrets. The persona of Liberace has stood the test of time and has been resurrected throughout the years because wrapped in the extravagance of one of America's most beloved and most recognized brands are the struggles we all understand, the successes we all hope to achieve and the legacy we all hope to build.

Bibliography

"Biography for Liberace." IMDB.
http://www.imdb.com/name/nm0508766/bio
accessed January 24, 2013.

Evans, KJ. "Walter Liberace The Music Man." *Las Vegas Review-Journal* 12 September 1999.
http://www.lvrj.com/1st100/part3/liberace.html accessed January 24, 2013.

Gaines, James R. "Liberace." *People* 4 October 1982.
http://www.people.com/people/archive/article/0,,20 083233,00.html accessed January 24, 2013.

"Good Morning America Covers Liberace's Death."
http://www.youtube.com/watch?v=3jN3WxAzTLs
accessed January 22, 2013.

"How did Liberace Die." Youtube segment from BBC's documentary *Too Much of a Good Thing is Wonderful.* **http://www.youtube.com/watch?v=q8WOoBmSc8 0** accessed January 22, 2013.

"How Liberace Became a Star." Youtube segment from BBC's documentary *Too Much of a Good Thing is Wonderful.* **http://www.youtube.com/watch?v=Se3sESeVoDY** accessed January 22, 2013.

"Interview with Scott Thorson." CNN's *Larry King Live* 12 August 2002. **http://transcripts.cnn.com/TRANSCRIPTS/0208/1 2/lkl.00.html accessed January 24**, 2013.

Jerry Goldbery discusses Liberace's childhood grow by Julie Lawrence. **http://www.onmilwaukee.com/podcast/podcast-166.html** accessed January 24, 2013.

Joslyn, Jay. "Liberace's Music and Flamboyant Life Earned him the Title Mr. Showmanship." *The Milwaukee Sentinel* 26 January 1990. **http://news.google.com/newspapers?nid=1368&da t=19900126&id=FqxRAAAAIBAJ&sjid=shIEAA AAIBAJ&pg=6349,6019749** accessed January 24, 2013.

"Liberace." Wikipedia.
http://en.wikipedia.org/wiki/Liberace accessed January 21, 2013.

"Liberace: The Milwaukee Maestro." Wisconsin Historical Society's *Magazine of History* Winter 2009 **http://www.povletichproductions.com/PovletichPr oductions/Writings/Entries/2009/12/1_Liberace__ The_Milwaukee_Maestro_- _Magazine_Article.html accessed January 24**, 2013.

"Liberace: Too much of a good thing is wonderful." Youtube segment from BBC's documentary *Too Much of a Good Thing is Wonderful.* **http://www.youtube.com/watch?v=zGh3jkb8zq8** accessed January 22, 2013.

"Liberace and the Girl Next Door." Youtube segment from BBC's documentary *Too Much of a Good Thing is Wonderful.* **http://www.youtube.com/watch?feature=endscree n&NR=1&v=xNmvkvm99iI** accessed January 22, 2013.

"Liberace had Last Laugh on Critics by 'Laughing all the way to the bank.'" *The Pittsburgh Press* 5 February 1987.
http://news.google.com/newspapers?id=lPgjAAAA IBAJ&sjid=L2MEAAAAIBAJ&pg=7055,2894925 &dq=liberace+denied+homosexual&hl=en
accessed January 24, 2013.

"Liberace Museum Closing."
http://www.roadsideamerica.com/story/2895
accessed January 23, 2013.

"Liberace Sues UK Newspaper." Youtube segment from BBC's documentary *Too Much of a Good Thing is Wonderful.*
http://www.youtube.com/watch?feature=endscree n&v=TLoLSa3qsuA&NR=1 Acccssed January 22, 2013.

"Liberace the Original Celebrity." Youtube segment from BBC's documentary *Too Much of a Good Thing is Wonderful.*
http://www.youtube.com/watch?v=lMg83t9mej0
accessed January 22, 2013.

"Liberace the Original Celebrity." Youtube segment from BBC's documentary *Too Much of a Good Thing is Wonderful.*
http://www.youtube.com/watch?v=lMg83t9mej0
accessed January 22, 2013.

"Liberace's Last Interview from TV Guide's Top 25 from OWN Network."
http://www.youtube.com/watch?NR=1&v=X7ox5 mQEZW8&feature=endscreen accessed January 22, 2013.

Nelson, Harry. "Liberace Died of Pneumonia Caused by AIDS, Riverside Coroner Reports." Los Angeles Times 10 February 1987.
http://articles.latimes.com/1987-02-10/local/me-2349_1_riverside-county-coroner accessed January 24, 2013.

Pyron, Darden Asbury. "The Days of the Understated Suit." *Liberace: An American Boyhttp://www.press.uchicago.edu/Misc/Chicago/686 671.html* accessed January 24, 2013

Solomon, Daina Beth. "Liberace." Los Angeles Times 16 June 2010.
http://projects.latimes.com/hollywood/star-walk/liberace/ accessed January 25, 2013.

Taylor Andrew. "Liberace Museum Sells Shoes Inspired by 'King of Bling." *Spring Valley View*.
http://www.viewnews.com/2008/VIEW-Jan-22-Tue-2008/SpringValley/19163172.html accessed January 24, 2013.

"The Secret Life of Liberace" on CNN's Larry King Live. **http://www.youtube.com/watch?v=dbMK3R770-Y** accessed January 22, 2013.

"What's With the Thousands Of Female Liberace Fans Who Call The Hennaed, Perfumed, Sequin-Jacketed Piano Player The Ideal American Man?" **http://www.bobsliberace.com/decades/1950s/qt.ht ml** accessed January 24, 2013.

Walsh,Mike. "The Weird, Wild, Wonderful Liberace." **http://www.missioncreep.com/mw/liberace.html** accessed January 24, 2013.

Welter, Ben. "Liberace Wins Libel Suit." *Star Tribune* 18 June 1959. **http://blogs2.startribune.com/blogs/oldnews/archi ves/70** accessed January 24, 2013.

Made in the USA
Lexington, KY
28 April 2014